DREAM OF XIBALBA

PRAISE

"*Dream of Xibalba* is a long and hypnotic meditation on rediscovery. Each page spirals out from the page before in a manner of breathless recognition: 'You open yourself / your mouth your eyes your forehead / with a sharp stone carried from childhood.' This is not a poetry of fearlessness but of the journey one takes in spite of fear. 'This is what you must listen for.'"

–**Jericho Brown**, judge of The 2021 Orison Poetry Prize

"A journey deep into ancestry and identity, the ties of blood and bone, *Dream of Xibalba* is rife with intricate and ancient symbolism. Adams-Santos deftly leads us on in mythic and transformational meditation on the ways in which we're formed by both the ghosts of our past and the rich tapestry of our present moment."

–**Jessica Hundley**

"The poemspace is often a dreamspace, whether in Homer or the *Popol Vuh*, the dream-visions of medievals, the post-Freudian associations of automatic writing, or even the aspirationalism of liberatory poetries. In all of these, though, the dreamspace is too a deathspace, with an underworld, an afterlife. In Stephanie Adams-Santos's *Dream of Xibalba*, this wide breadth of dreamspace is acutely a deathspace, enabling a poetry as equally imaginative as material, mythic as personal. Alongside the one world of prosaic light and knowledge, it imagines 'another world of life and death,' 'another blood,' 'another memory nested / in memory.' Past the prosaic, horizontal certainties of waking life, *Dream of Xibalba* reaches— downward, upward—to 'names you've forgotten,' 'names you never knew.'"

–**Jos Charles**

"In this vivid book-length poetic sequence in 12 parts, Stephanie Adams-Santos investigates the fraught, elusive territory where memory and history intersect with presence, and landscape is haunted by dream and disappearance. Here is a world where a long-dead ancestor is 'forever burning in place,' a bird nips 'at its own shadow,' and 'There is nothing here / that will tell you who you are.'"

–**Laurie Sheck**

DREAM OF
XIBALBA

a poem

Stephanie Adams-Santos

Dream of Xibalba

ISBN: 978-1-949039-38-2

Orison Books
PO Box 8385
Asheville, NC 28814
www.orisonbooks.com

Distributed to the trade by Itasca Books
(952) 223-8373 / orders@itascabooks.com

Custom cover art by Ricardo Cavolo. www.ricardocavolo.com

Manufactured in the U.S.A.

ORISON
BOOKS

CONTENTS

Dice el tecolote
tuu-kuru ku ku, tuu-kuru ku ku

Hay días que amanezco muy triste . . .
Saber por que. Saber que será.

tuu-kuru ku ku, tuu-kuru ku ku
Así dicen los tecolotes.

The owl says
tuu-kuru ku ku, tuu-kuru ku ku

There are days I wake up with such a sadness . . .
Who can say why. Who can say what for.

tuu-kuru ku ku, tuu-kuru ku ku
So the owls say.

–Amanda Consuelo García (1930–2018)

In the night sky is a road
which begins in the center of
Earth.

As above, so below.

In the mouth's bower
the roses of Xibalba flare.

One

At the first altar of blood
there was hardly a sound
but a trembling, something in the earth,

a murmuring of teeth and mycelia,
simple cries—

                    ayyy ayyy

sounds moving like slugs in the grass
of the body, leaving traces of memory,
the slow sound of the earth digesting.

This is what you must listen for.

The sounds that spill from the hands
and burrow deep into earth,
thickening in syrups, growing old and silent.
Fossils do not only live in stone.

The shape within you pushes outward.

There beyond the torrent
is the entrance to the underworld,
marked by an abundance of water
that asserts itself in blood

y olor de los caites perdidos . . .

You try to crawl inside
but are too thick with supplication,

too wet with the rains
of your past—

you are drunk!

The forms of your heart
converge and flatten like a clumsy shield.

You stumble past into dryness, stuck in the world,
though your blood remains
both here and there.

Daughter of Xibalba

your eye of water is drowned,
lost in its vessel of clay.

Olla roja—hueco
con olor de los ríos.

You are banished,
your heart a mist

outside of your body,
ash after a fire.

Flowers at your feet like pools of night.

You reach into the folds
as into the shadows of your reflection.

The mountain stirs.

La Sierra de los Cuchumatanes
susurra, allí donde andan los cazadores
de los loros . . .

Here again is a mythos of blood,
thoughts filling & emptying
as water from a vase.

Green water, black water,
flickering, blank—

Water without reflection, water that smells of death,
warm as the tears that draw trails of light
from your spectral breast.

Remembering, forgetting,
you flare into being.

You go to the window
to see what time it is—

now the black grass

has eaten the heads of the flowers,
the amethyst of sky
is dim,

full of ash without origin.

Before dawn your eyes emerge,
a bird there
nipping at its own shadow,
vision doubled and burnt.

You loiter by the cabinet
of the quetzal, inside
the one candle burns to a nub.

You anoint yourself
with the mute tallow and the
air thickens around you.

There is nothing here
that will tell you who you are.

Outside the water sings
its tortuous note,
devoid of the parrot,
devoid of the quetzal.

A song without ears,
a dry silk wrapped around the throat,
neither warm nor cold
but the vacillation
between them.

A hammer swings
through the aether of the flesh,
the mind's red line.

Tonight a part of you shivers, liking it,
your whole body in one place,
where steel drags along.

You wonder if now the body wants more
to open or to shut.

Two

chh chh chh

The hens tear open the earth
with their sun-colored hands.

Wake up!

There are rumors about you
the Strangers pass amongst themselves.

They don't know,
they don't know

pain is a flower
that blooms in the eye.

Unable to sleep
you go adrift from your house of nerves.

Between your eyes and the ceiling
a recollection comes.

You are the gossamer prisoner
spun into the shape of what you see.

Angular, without pattern,
like a headache hanging in air,

scent of nose-blood and damp ash,
a crystal shattered in stone.

Perfume of the underworld,
homeward as a hammer's head.

A psychic weight
tumbles in the shade of the magnolia.

Two eyes are buried,
two stones at your feet.

Here you stand
in the infinite dreaming of the dead.

Objects shed their illusions.

The bottle of rum,
the bottle of whiskey.
Now both are folded into blood.

A note in your grandmother's hand
passes to yours,

blank, deep red.

You're trying to remember something . . .

the fearful neutrality
of a rose
without moisture.

You can't explain it to anyone
but in the back of your mind

a brittle rose hangs
upside down

swinging above you
in the past

without a shadow.

Kukulkan sleeps, steeped in earth,
a black root thickening with spice.

Why should you lie?
It's not god you're thinking of.

You lean to touch your wife
who isn't there.

Your tongue becomes foam
and morning makes a paste of your eyes
on the metate stone.

Three

Tendrils propagate from your bones,
searching for something to cling to.

If only you could pray the right way
you might reach the secret sleep
of the creator where the roses
engulf you.

If you had the right words
you could taste the whole earth
with this vacant tongue.

It's as though you are walking alone
in a garden. Out of the sky,

the star cuts you.

You hear the crush of flowers,
a sharp cry, the obsecration of a stem.

The blood in your body   has lost itself
& turned to water.

                You pertain to your sorrow.
                You are invented by its blows.

                Far away, a single rose
swelling on the vine—

the old thing humming
just freshly born

        Blue shadow, absolute.

Can a shape look like a cry?
Can't joy erupt from a thorn?

You are netted by ghosts—O shadowy aunts of Xinabajul
        who talk beneath ruins, O basket-headed women
of Huehuetenango, who fill the graveyard ovens with bread,

the white-earth mouths of the ovens, the blue-tongued heat
        hisses silently at their hands.

You walk at night to the stone court of Zaculeu,
        dreaming of the stone ball falling that obliterates the nerves.

You climb the temple stairs, climb arduously
        toward Death.

        Off the wet edge of obsidian
your head tumbles down the arc of a serpent's back
        singing!—

Stone that swallows blood
                        O temple catch me catch me

You want to know where you come from.

Aquí la noche da vueltas lentas

un zopilote
        negro e inmenso

The night circles you
        with its many eyes of fire.

Below you the ground
        is a vast accumulation.

You scry into an emptiness
                where everything blinks back,

        a thousand bodies of memory
buzzing through darkness,
                        a great swarm

that descends, eating the violets, lilies, aguacates . . .

        All reflections consumed, the eclipse cuts even
your shadow.
                You are the lost daughter of Xibalba.

Can't you see the scythe
                swinging from your footsteps,

        a thousand deaths in every direction?

Beneath you
amethyst caves vibrate and groan
the earth's emptiness.

Mushrooms of pleasure
molt into dark cupolas.

Now a shade falls over you, a chittering—
infinitesimal spirits too slight for understanding.

You open yourself,
your mouth your eyes your forehead
with a sharp stone carried from childhood.

The owl,
fastened like the moon against the night,
is pale, intent on your sorrow.

A vine climbs the darkness up.

Blooms invert, huecos florecidos . . .

Before you disappear, a disfiguring music
comes in the form of a hummingbird
who mistakes your eye for a flower.

You follow a vision of birds,
a wet slope down to the river.

You forget about desire,
stand there staring at the greenish silt.

It's a dream,
everything floating over,
lazy, going by . . .

But someone in the lace of flames
screams far away,

another world of life and death,

another city, another blood.
Another memory nested
in memory.

Your chest aches like a bomb, asleep

Four

Outside, a pale figure
crosses the Terrero.

A shape
aimless & tainted
with the smell of hens, the smell of water.

You sense a softness
like the veil of a bride
        cascading down a woman's back,
obscuring the swordplay of her eyes.

The figure walks
with backward feet, cabezona de caballo,
        los ojos dos cenotes
llenos de sal.

She walks the sacrament of your memory
backward into shadow, her white tulle fluttering
into the past.

Behind the temple of Zaculeu
her long tail darkens the ground.

Now the window is blank.

Turning back to the stove, you remember
your grandmother's words—

don't turn your back on the masa, on the fire, on the dead

Here is that old feeling again.
That nearly senseless body floating over your body.

That specter, la siguanaba de tu sangre,
projected from the prism of your skeleton.

Milk spills from the voids of its eyes,
risen from the tributaries of its perished breasts.

Beneath the vale of its hair, you're immobile,
wet from its weeping, your face washed

and eyes made white, lips flush
against the lace of baptism.

The ache slides from one side to the other,
cargo from another time. It rests at your hips,
a smoldering stone, but cold. Now a serpent
licks the backs of your eyes, with the thin blue flame
of its desire. Your spirit shivers away from your bones.

The presence of a murdered woman

commands an empty sensation.

A correspondence—

a sudden nameless tug.

Ghosts are immortal feelings.

The forest burns, inner lives and past
wrinkling in the ferns—

you can't hurry your eyes
from the sigil of light that binds them.

From your brain the colors
seep down,

come like magma
into the cool cavity of your chest,

shatter and darken
to obsidian.

Severed at the stalk of utterance,

you kiss the air.

You kiss the creases
of your hands,

but it's Agony
whose tongue
enters you.

In the middle of your body
the dream is coming.

In the petrified loom
a figure burns in the weft.

Alone in her house
your great grandmother is engulfed in skirts of fire.

The past walks in circles
inside you—

a corpse with backward feet,
a loop of herself, weaving herself,

      remembering herself

inside another body.

You can speak a little bit
of Spanish,

but a lost language
sits on your tongue.

A toad
the weight of stone.

Black and green from the river.

Fulgent, the perfume
of its flesh.

If you speak now
you'll lisp, you'll hiss.

Five

Cherubs their
big eyes gleam
and the moon
blue on their
bare heads
the color of night
they climb
down the darkness
through the
bedroom window
to see you
to touch you
light in their hands
light in their eyes

A small man in the jungle of Tikal
　　　　blesses himself with leopard's dung.

In the shade of an achiote shrub.
　　　　he makes his cheeks red,

Under your pillow, he leaves a mirror,
a slab of black stone
　　　　　while you dream,

an opening that never closes.

The old women of your head walk in procession,

　　　　　　　endlessly coming

　　　　　　　　　　　and going.

You've heard of flowers
    growing from nothing,
standing up on stone,
    sucking blood from the sunlight.
Far away the mountains
    conspire with their ghosts.
The fossils beneath
    still cradle the empty forms.
The psyches where have they gone?
    Even extinction has its children.

In total darkness
bursts of jasmine float into flesh.

In the midnight heat
the sun keeps its hands on you.

In the florid orgasm,
in tomorrow's light
far away,

you see yourself only faintly.

At this hour
you lie beneath slabs of noise,

helicopter blades
cutting the dark
high above you.

A cat's cry unravels in air,
in wind, the bruised grasses
hissing, all sounds tangling
in the hands of obscurity.

Pressed to your window
you look madly for proof.
But there is none.

The pant of a dog
or coyote propagates a flower.

The bright red head
of sleep floats to your breast.

You dream all night
of the room beneath your room,
that bed made of water.

You dream the ground
shakes open, a rift
full of flowers.

The enormous blooms
swallow your head,

thorns bud from the stalks
of your limbs.

Light pools up behind the dam.

Still you wither in this bed

until at last something moves—
the roots shake and sigh
                    unwitnessed.

My wife, are you nowhere?

Kukulkan is waking.

Stepping out of the dream,
you must carry the sight
        of the god alone.

You write a few things down
every day, you throw salt
into the sink.

It all dissolves.

Your flesh beneath a veil
caresses a void.

Two vultures,
each eat at the site of the other's dissolution.

Between them words flay the air
& come back wet.

Heads of thunder, red.

A scrawl glistens in the book of the body.

One eye weeps, washing itself.
The other dreams.

Here and there
a figure climbs high into the air,
teetering on the edge—

a siren,
a slash of red
burning through time.

A moan hangs in the sky,
a remora of clouds.

At a certain hour when you pass behind the house
the young turkeys will melt into shadows
and you will see the long white veils of the dead,
their glimmering slimes that reflect green light
and the pale flesh that breathes in the darkness of melons.

The moon who lives underground
will tug at your feet, pulling them backward.

Midday smoke closes the sky, where the sun becomes the moon,
a primitive eye, illegible gaze that blurs and possesses, passing over
broken sigils strewn on the ground, the arms of trees
voided wands torn open for the dreaming of fire, fed by a bestial wind,
wind that sucks the whines from a wrinkle in the air,
wind that drinks blood from the spirit's eye.

Feral children howling in cages call back to the coyotes
that descend from the hills, back and forth, their hunger and delirium,
back and forth the fire and the wind, the furnace and ash,
the long road home, this season of fire.

Six

At night a woman crosses the courtyard with her hair down

like a pelt. She smells of the river, and jade that throbs underground,

green brood in a womb of stone. A lonely, violet perfume.

A bone-smell. In the soft shuffling of her backward feet

is the music of a past life, a nostalgia for living, a lullaby

that rides sharp and high through the nose, piercing the brain

to come home.

You fall into habits
of sadness,

how could you not,

with the burning rose
that shrieks through
your soul?

A vestigial rope grows from your head,
whipping the air with lashes.

You try to lop it off,
give it back to the baleful star.

But it lives,
hauling its own wet life
from the brink.

Past an impenetrable oval
(a painting of a rose)

a single window
opens and closes,

the sound of a wing.

You go from room to room
without feet.

Is the pain inside or out?

In the night, teeth are thrown across the floor.
Your pre-columbian memories, stelaes of bone, they fall across the bed.
Toothless, you lie without limbs, head grown on a stalk without pith.
Your gaze falling toward the skylight where a red tunnel closes in.
It begins to rain. Sorrow wafts from the ceiling fan
filling the room with fog.

In the morning you crawl over broken pieces, piercing your knees,
your hands, your tongue, you make holes in your thoughts,
make windows and doors and other stations of oblivion.

You hear the crush of leaves,
someone walking alone

where the old garden
once had roses.

Now the aphids are carved on stone
buried underfoot, stelae of a dead afternoon.

A child parts the dry grass
on its belly, without feet,
coming toward.

Someone calls you from the house,
not your mother, not your grandmother—
your secret name tolling like a bell.

A scent of melons and milk,
a scent of yesterday, calling . . .

By night you walk, not knowing what you have.
Such demons in the margins. You lift shadows
from the page, raise glyphs crumbling
from gutturals, dirtying your hands, little
poem of adobe, palabras de lodo y agua sucia . . .
The new moon makes a needle of itself,
as if to say *give me your tongue.*
This is what piercings are for.

Surely the gossip of hens
                is a language of death.

      Xibalba chirps near a hole in the ground.

There, if you listen, is the sound of all animals
      arcane beneath the aria of silence.

An animal of sadness
swings its head in the dark,
behind the house,

without a name,
the gate groans.

You're far from your
mother's garden.

Gusts of noise
pull the eyelids back
from the flowers.

Gripped in your dreaming
      you can only listen.

      Somewhere in the dunes
             is a wall aflame.

Sombras llegando, sombras partiendo . . .

   A thousand doors
         melting shut,
              red doors, obscene doors.

Sombras llegando, sombras partiendo.

   Just their screams left behind,
burrowing into earth.

Your eyes are wearing down,

eyes so thin the copper road
shines behind them.

Your irises waver

like dandelion tufts,
conspiring with air.

But your pupils
tunnel back into your skull
like clams, down, down,
they emerge blind at your feet.

You wonder

when will the hurled stone
finally break
          the edge of your heaven

and where will it bury its head
when it lands

          and if it is a seed
                    what type of seed—

puffing out from its germ in the dark?

At dinner you find a slick gray stone
floating in your soup,

                the heart of a hen
en el caldo, un espejo.
        You turn, not wanting to see
                      a woman in white
who crosses the courtyard, hollow-eyed,
        mumbling her ballad of the machete—

                mi marido me quitó las manos
           mi marido me quitó la cabeza

    Her body trails behind her
in the shape of a dog.

Flesh rings like a telephone,
traveling body to body
on the night's cord.

Hurt comes
spilling through the open line.

Each voice falls braided
to the bottom of the well,
thick and black as a horse's tail.

You live there
under the weight of old water.

You live there.

Seven

In the tunnels beneath Zaculeu,
you put on the sleep of a mongrel.

A secret perfume
touched to the fold of each eye.

Out into the day, under the sun,
you wear the dog's glistering tears.

Touched in each eye with the rheum of a dog,
a sixth sense opens, una tela oscura, hecho de miradas lejanas,
a clandestine cloth woven from time.

Now stains of the past come alive in the air,
sharp against your nostrils.

Blooms of rot & huele-a-noche, shapes you couldn't see before.

Handprints on a wall, moaning forms that float through the house,
fossils of anguish, recuerdos del machete.

You dreamt of a girl in the desert between two moons.

She wore two masks—one of broken teeth, the other made of leaves.

The ground was rotten at her feet, it moved, unfolding, inviting as a bed.
Beneath the masks a bit of water gurgled over stone, the sky a reflection
of water.

Water in her hands.
Water in the river of her gaze.

Soft light and a vulture's shadow lay over you both.
A flower floated at her breast, pale blue, transparent.
An eye
            sleeping in tulle.

Copal is wept from trees.

Lágrimas doradas crecidas en las sombras
de la sierra.

Copal of your mother's country,
copal of her earliest memory,
of her childhood land
nestled at the foot of mountains
near the ruined city of white earth
and ash and the echoes of stone.

Copal is the blood of the trees.

Sangre ámbar rezumando sobre la memoria.

Past the armful of lilies
en el cuartecito azul,

the smoldering corner
all full of smoke,

your grandmother kneels
before the two christs.

Black twins of sorrow,
silver and lace

fanning from the grace of their heads,
and a golden garland strung between them.

Señores de esquipulas,
suffused with incense

and the soot of prayers
spoken from burning mouths,

they point to all corners of the earth,
inward and outward.

In the Laguna de Ocubilá,
　　the dead are only asleep.

Bone is to stone an old memory.

In the land of the turtles,
　　　bones are carried back.

Look, beyond the orchard of aguacates
　　the flowers of a shrine

open their mouths, their yellow eyes.

An angel is coming . . .

Sounds fold and warp,
flitting across the night
like shadows of bats
come to roost in the grottos.
Behind your sleepless eyes
the chatter of a woman
whose skirts caught fire,
your great grandmother
who died like a tree,
forever burning in place.
Her eyeless wings sweep over you.

Bent in prayer, the body
        is an arc of listening,

rainbow of incarnate light
      leaning toward the groaning of gods

and whispers of beheading. The beating of drums
      circular in blood rhythms.

    How hens scratch at the earth
 searching for something to kill,

and when the air is golden
          with vibrations

   and annihilation rings
        in their clawed hands, they

   tear open the floor,
        call up the green, soft genesis of the worm.

Your carnal eyes,
two agates

suspended in murk.
The river's soft silt,

life passing by overhead.
A murmur, a dream.

Emerging from underground
you nearly step into
the sleek red pool of a crime scene.

Sound eats sound,
a silence made of noise,

where a metal bar
opened a man's head.

The little person of your spirit
slips out to see, all wide open—
the wraith of someone's pain.

Stalk of flesh,
bystander,

your blood communes
with the blood on the street,
turning cold in remembrance.

The water comes in leaden sheets. You're struck
down and down again until you are beneath it. The bed is made
above you, the firm sheets pinned to the edge. A voice says it is time
to sleep, *duerme con los angelitos.* You see a light that burns
your eyes, the birthplace of parrots.

Eight

Pashtuda, despierta. At your mother's voice you come awake.
You open, sliding to the edge. *Pon los pies en el suelo.*

You lie down in hellish grass.

The blank faces regard you, buried far beneath, words carved
from a twin emptiness. You crawl toward an altar of stone.
Over a gold-hammered bowl, you let go of your blood, you make room.

The bed creaked and you woke. Sunlight
the color of lilies spilled over the sheets,
an absent color,
leaned over the bed to kiss you. An insect
trembled on the windowsill, warming itself,
then flew, but its tiny thoughts grew swollen
in your mind, where your skull throbbed
with magnification. A hum from deep
in the throat of God scraped over your body.
A dry sound, followed by the obfuscation of a stream.
You felt your chest split open
and colors floating out
like petals,
       blue, turquoise, green,

               puffs of violet . . .

One day in the garden
a door in your chest
swings open,

a shadow flies out—

Your mother's memory
of chasing vultures
by the Seleguá—

Her feet bare, the color of dust.

Wings glide over the roses,
over your hands.

Sombras tiernas de los zopilotes.

Suffused with sleep, you exit
    from your shape.

Arrastrándose de un hueco
        al fondo de tus recuerdos . . .

    Birds pass over you.
            Seeds and ordure fall
down the bright sky.

    Tan sencillo el aire . . .

You enter the flayed house,

muscling your way
                        to the kitchen
against a horde of raw silences.

Your mother turns toward you.
Your grandmother turns toward you.
The Burning One turns toward you.

    Spirit erects in the tongue,
all blood rushing to the mouth . . .

    Warm tortillas, dusted with salt,
        ground chili and vapors of lime.

Your tongue, the serpent,
leads you home to yourself.

Zopilote, Zopilote—

In your childhood ear
the word sounds like *sopa* & *elote*—
soup & corn, elements of a future-body.

Black soup, black corn,
warm in the cazuela.

You scavenge the things of memory.

Bright red head of chile molido,
crushed on the metate stone.

Lime, salt—

The god opens its wings
behind your teeth.

A shadow goes along the floor
on its way, slowly, to bed.

Light pulls back, unreachable,
uncovering the emptiness of the tomb,
    that little room just behind the ribs.

The demon there, staked to stone
seems pitiful.

You close the shutters.
You close the windows, the doors.

You close your hands.
Between them the nothingness flinches,
wrinkling its vast body.

Nine

The shadows
    between the roses

fall over the earth.

    It seems the mouths are all open

and between these aisles of breath,
    a stranger wanders.

The sky is getting black beyond you,
where it will rain.

Where you will again be baptized
with your own name

and you will wash the blood and the day from your face.

In your dream, the animals turned against the people.
    You were one of them, yellow-eyed.

Terrible forms walked on all fours, without blood
    and hard, unremembering faces, blank as dandelions.

You clawed the whites from their gazes and
    clipped their blonde heads from their shoulders.

It rained a while. The sky hunched on its knees
    scrubbing the floor.

A music of toads filled the house. They slid beneath the door
    and swam into the courtyard and into your bedroom

where you had slipped into the green
    of the swamp like a velvet dress, back into blankness,

full of rest, turning softer and softer, a slime,
    dreaming no longer, but the dream itself.

Sky was dark with passage,
the ocean crawling above you.

An old music, an old memory.

You leaned against your window
to the sound of falling—

rain, yes, but something else as well,

far away, something burning—

the last of its kind.

Look around you. Here are the skeletal temples of Zaculeu,
or the ghost of the old house that once stood on the hill,
the place your mother sat beneath el viejo jocotal,
alive before you ever existed, an owl above her
in the hollow, living too beyond the span of its body.

Beetle of the blast,
of the badland, you
scud over these wastes
speak over these wastes
sing over these wastes—
a clap in the bone
your presence strikes
your song rings
through all the bodies
all the bones—
the garden rises
ah, who would guess
it is yours all yours
that you
would inherit the earth
that you
had such visions in you

Ten

Kneel and carve your bones
with all symbols of night.

Not jasmine, not fireflies,

the other Night.

The thin chirps
of a spider monkey
in a neighbor's yard

calls for something in the trees.

Not hunger, not thirst.

There's hardly a sound
as you lean all the way into darkness,
through the heavy leaves,
through the loam.

Night of the Hands.
Night of the Eyes.
Eclipse of the Flesh.

Your head goes to seed tonight, a numb sound,
thoughts weakly beating down to the ground,
the dogs watching silently, ears pricked.

This is the sabbath of the body. You have no wife,
no lover. You are only a stem, a bend in the breeze.
Innocence flutters away, a leaf from a tree.
Look where its edges find the earth and leave no trace.

Sky fulfills an entrance to the body.
One body fills with another.

Body takes of body.

Again the lightlessness inside
asserts the Rose.

The sky comes eagerly.
parting your lips.
Where the riverbed swells

and moves to your breast,
lilies tremble open
toward the star.

From their mouths a lacy sorrow
collapses, and

a hush buzzes in the hollow,
the thickness of a hummingbird,

the shape of a syllable in the mouth,
just before the word . . .

In a field,
a little acupuncture of light
pushes toward the rosebuds

of your eyes, undoing the burrs
of your stubborn lips,
your stubborn face.

The grass eclipses
the wreck of your heart
& the names of things

crawl away on long feet,
blind & slow
leaving only traces.

In the morning you walk away from it all,
moving bone by bone past the bush
where the white burning flares
of the flower-bodies live.

Where else would you hope to mend
were it not for this green-blooded bower
far from the walls of the house, away
from perfection and all her porcelain forms?

You are beautiful as you are.
Ragged as the leaves that are beginning
to turn, some falling, some still
holding on, staggering each day into life.

O creature of the garden, it is all
already inside you.

Eleven

Most days you move like a ship.

Blood over the desert.

The rolls of your back
slope like the dunes themselves.

When you lie down

the softness startles you,
your nakedness conversing with the elements.

A sadness fans out
into carnal shapes—

the crystal habit of the rose.

The specter rides in you.
A long white ribbon
suckled to your mist.

You know you ought to tear it out
and kill it once and for all.

You ought to crawl again toward the bed,
make your way back
to the one who loves you,

to her sturdy hands
and her strong, tattooed arms
that hold the pillows down
as if you were there.

But a shape in the living room
unfolds like a screen.

You are lit with emptiness.

You stay with it, nowhere,
hooked to where you stand.

A spiral peels open in you,
without dimension.
You stay with it

until morning comes
to spit you out.

You hoof your way up the temple stairs
in a cloak of burrs.

Light slashes its own stem,
throws a bouquet of vicious color
across the sky.

The moon is looking.

Go slow now,
don't run or it will chase you.

Day and night you carve a circle
from stone,

comiendo la casa de barro

on the hill where no one can see you.

Gnawing and grinding, taking unto yourself
the adobe that tastes of flesh,
the splendor of dirt.

You consume the old house,

flesh without sorrow.

Your swollen head suckles
at the stars, filled with the glinting
blue fire of the dead.

In the kitchen
masa lifts on the fire,
little faces of the moon
shaped by someone else's hands.

A burning angel
feeds at the shadows there,

a smell of white lilies from the corner of the room.

Twelve

Fuego de matapalos, fuego verde. Red light of birth.
Blank light of death. You wrench yourself ajar
to the first blow, the first memory, a primal contusion.
You read by touch, sigils in offal grumbling in the living cavern
where past lives grow, ensconsed in flesh. Your eyes are sealed,
muted, the obsidian veils of a mirror hewn from stone.
Upon your fingers a text blackens, cutting, as you open
to the book of flowers, flores milagrosas que brotan en sangre.
The sierra whispers into your feet, a voice of crushed stone.
Step forward half in sleep, into the capilla of the midnight eye.

One day you'll return to the place of the parrots.
Un-hunt them, give back the depths of their eyes.

A toad sings from your tongue, vanishing into water.
Green and brown, then black, swimming into shadows.

From the sole of each foot, two stelae grow upright
bearing the names you've forgotten. The names you never knew.

Only an insect
persists in the yard.

Unseen for the dark,
its black chirr
waves invisibly between us,

A veil of anguish
enfolding our kiss.

Kukulkan parts the grass
behind you.

A velvet meat
breathes, the Past

which has no eyes
blindly nudges along.

Outside the house
is the feathery perfume of plantain,
bitter caramel of dead leaves.
The memories you carry.

Tomorrow maybe,
the god's dark head will crown from the wound.

Step forward into darkness again,
where demons' paper wings
wave bright kites from altars of the void.

The sun's orphaned roots recite the throbbing vowels
of a nest into your hands. Trace a clutch of eggs,
golden beneath your tongue.

A blue flame in the hearth of all your memories,
untouchable germ of remembrance.
One foot pierces the world below, and the other rests firm above.

May the green sword of the angel guide your feet.
Know the holy sting of its touch.

When the locust comes to the window
you must let your blood move to each side,
making a path. It's okay if you have nothing to sing.

Sensation walks through you.

It's okay to lie still,
to let the blooming happen all around you.

You will be good again
when the flimsy grass pierces the earth.

ACKNOWLEDGMENTS

A book is a small boat held afloat by a great sea. I'm so grateful to all who have upheld me and my work through this process of creation.

Thank you to Jericho Brown for seeing into the core of this work and selecting it for The 2021 Orison Poetry Prize. Thank you to Luke Hankins, editor of Orison Books, for being a most wonderful partner in the journey of shepherding these pages into a real-life book. Thank you to the incomparable Ricardo Cavolo for such bright, exquisite artwork on the cover.

Thank you to Jos Charles, Jessica Hundley, and Laurie Sheck for your deep reading, and offering your time and natural brilliance to shaping such incisive interpretations of the book.

Thank you to the following people and publications for publishing portions of this manuscript: *Orion* (via Camille Dungy); *Iterant Magazine* (via Walter Stone & Candace Jenson); *Gaze Journal* (via Darla Mottram); The Academy of American Poets (via Samiya Bashir); *Até Mais: Until More, An Anthology of Latinx Futurisms* from Vellum Books (via editors Kim Sousa, Malcom Friend, & Alan Chazaro).

Thank you to Vermont Studio Center for awarding me a Henry David Thoreau Fellowship. A large and important portion of this book came into form in the early spring of 2019 as I watched the river slowly thawing from the window of my VSC studio. Thank you to the Regional Arts and Culture Council (RACC) for helping to make travel to that residency possible.

Thank you to Trio House Press for selecting this manuscript as a semi-finalist for The 2021 Louise Bogan Award and to Black Springs Press for counting it on the shortlist for The 2021 Sexton Prize. These encouragements go a long way.

Thank you to those eagle-eyed readers and dear friends whose generous readings and reflections helped strengthen my clarity and belief in the final form of this book: Elsa Gomez (mi flor), Harper Quinn, Kelsi Schwetz, Mike Soto.

Thank you to my creative community whose words, advice, work, spirit, and support has nourished and bolstered my spirit, creatively and otherwise: Intisar Abioto, Maryanna Aster, Apoorva Charan, Roland Dahwen, Mayra Douglas, Grace Evangelista, Jack Gendron, Laura Goode, Jasmine Jaisinghani, Michelle Ruiz Keil, Lucy Luna, Rammy Park, Vera Miao, Nazli Rahmanian, Sam Roxas-Chua 姚, Michelle Sam, Gracie Simonette, Coleman Stevenson, Dao Strom, Katherine Sullivan, Stacey Tran . . . and my students past and present who inspire so many new questions and paths into listening and seeing.

Thank you to mi amor, Robin Sola, whose eyes are the final gate of all my projects, whose pure heart I can measure all truths against.

Thank you to my parents, Steve and Alma Adams, and my siblings Anna Griffin and Patrick Adams, whose endless love and imagination have forged the foundation of all that I am. Y gracias a tí, Gramita linda, por acompañarme en todos los caminos. Vives eternamente en mi corazón.

Finally, thank you to the great masters whose words live in me, who helped shape this book through the subterranean waters of psyche: Eunice Odio, Clarice Lispector, Ferenc Juhasz, Nelly Sachs, Lucille Clifton, Xavier Villarutia, Marisa di Giorgio, Alejandra Pizarnik . . .

ABOUT THE AUTHOR

Stephanie Adams-Santos's work spans poetry, prose, and screenwriting. She is the author of the full-length poetry collection *Swarm Queen's Crown* (a Lambda Literary Award finalist), as well as the chapbooks *Total Memory* and *The Sundering* (New York Chapbook Fellowship, Poetry Society of America). Her short story "Night Flowers" appeared in the Latinx anthology *Speculative Fiction for Dreamers*. Adams-Santos has served as Staff Writer and Story Editor on the television anthology horror series *Two Sentence Horror Stories* (CW/Netflix). Her episode "Elliot" won a 2022 Gold Telly Award in Writing. As an inaugural fellow of The 2022 Ojalá Ignition Fellowship, she developed an original fantasy pilot based on the world and characters of the Tarot. Most recently, she was a fellow of The 2022 Sundance Episodic Lab, developing an animated dystopian sci-fi/fantasy pilot. In addition to her literary work, Adams-Santos is a professional Tarot reader and is making headway on an original Major Arcana tarot deck inspired by occult animism.

ABOUT ORISON BOOKS

Orison Books is a 501(c)3 non-profit literary press focused on the life of the spirit from a broad and inclusive range of perspectives. We seek to publish books of exceptional poetry, fiction, and non-fiction from perspectives spanning the spectrum of spiritual and religious thought, ethnicity, gender identity, and sexual orientation.

As a non-profit literary press, Orison Books depends on the support of donors. To find out more about our mission and our books, or to make a donation, please visit www.orisonbooks.com.

Orison Books thanks Francisco Aragón
for his financial support of this title.

For information about supporting upcoming Orison Books titles,
please visit www.orisonbooks.com/donate,
or write to Luke Hankins at editor@orisonbooks.com.